Time Management

Optimize Your Potential! Established Strategies That Will Enable You To Attain Higher Levels Of Achievement And Efficiency

(The Ability To Regulate One's Emotions Effectively And Overcome Inertia)

Gerald Jauk

TABLE OF CONTENT

Understanding Time 1

Fewer Distractions From One's Coworkers Overall 8

Misconceptions That Are Widespread Debunked 18

Cultivating A Mentality Of Growth And Expansion 24

Developing An Individualised Timetable While Creating An Effective Time Management System 30

How To Take Charge Of Your Day By Creating An Efficient To-Do List 37

Strategies For Increasing One's Own Productivity 45

Establishing Crystal-Clear Objectives And Priorities 47

Establishing Crystal-Clear Objectives And Priorities 50

Prioritization, As Well As The Establishment Of Goals 62

Acquire Command Of Your Own Time. 70

Does Every Action You Take Essentially Become An Ongoing Struggle To Keep Pace? .. 89

Both Putting Things Off And Avoiding Them .. 92
The Realities And The Unrealistic Predictions 97
The Practice Of Effective Time Management 109
Implementing The Pomodoro Methodology For Efficient Time Allocation 122
Blocking Out Time 131
Acquiring An Understanding Of The Why 143
The Benefits Of Effective Time Management 155

Understanding Time

The Nature of Time

The concept of time is both intriguing and multifaceted, exerting its influence across various facets of our existence.

Although time is an inherently objective parameter, our subjective perception of it exhibits considerable variations.

At times, the fleeting nature of time can be apparent, while at other instances, it may be characterized by a slow and plodding pace.

This phenomenon can be attributed to the strong correlation between our activities, emotions, and circumstances, and the manner in which we observe and perceive the passage of time.

The principle of relativity pertaining to time exhibits the subjectivity inherent within its nature.

During the occurrence of an enjoyable or thrilling endeavor, time has a tendency to elapse swiftly, almost inconspicuously to our senses.

Conversely, during periods of boredom or while engaged in repetitive tasks, the perception of time can appear to decelerate.

This subjective apprehension of time underscores the significance of imbuing our experiences with significance and captivation in order to maximize the value of each passing instant.

Moreover, it is imperative to acknowledge that time is a limited and irreplaceable asset.

Each individual is allotted precisely 24 hours per day, with no additional or subtracted minutes.

The manner in which we elect to utilize this invaluable time significantly influences our efficiency, individual satisfaction, and overall well-being.

Recognizing and comprehending the transient quality of time is a fundamental initial measure towards enhancing the stewardship of this invaluable asset.

3

Setting Meaningful Goals

The establishment of purposeful objectives constitutes a fundamental component of proficient time allocation and organization. By establishing precise and well-defined objectives, we enhance our ability to effectively manage our time and actively strive towards attaining our intended results. Presented below are a set of instructions for establishing purposeful objectives.

1. Determine your objective: The initial stride towards establishing purposeful objectives is to determine your ambition. What are your objectives? What is the end objective you hope to achieve? Gaining clarity about your purpose can aid you in establishing precise and attainable objectives that are in harmony with your overarching vision.

2. Exercise precision: While establishing goals, it is imperative to articulate them with specificity. Unclear or extensive objectives can pose challenges in their attainment and may fail to offer distinct guidance for one's endeavors. Conversely, establish precise and quantifiable objectives that you can monitor and assess progressively. As an

illustration, rather than establishing a general objective of "getting in shape," opt for a precisely defined goal, such as "completing a 5km run in less than 30 minutes by the conclusion of the year."

3. Analyze your objectives: Analyzing your objectives by dividing them into smaller, feasible tasks enhances their attainability and aids in sustaining motivation. Ascertain the precise actions requisite to accomplish your objective, and establish strict timelines for each individual task. As an illustration, if your objective is to compose a literary work, it would be advantageous to deconstruct it into more manageable stages such as organizing the chapters, composing a designated quantity of words on a daily basis, and meticulously revising each individual chapter.

4. Ensure that your goals strike a balance between being ambitious and

attainable: The act of setting goals that are either excessively simple or overly challenging has the potential to interfere with your drive and result in feelings of frustration. Alternatively, establish objectives that present a meaningful level of difficulty while remaining attainable. Take into account your existing skills and resources, and establish objectives that challenge you beyond your usual limits but are still attainable.

5. Record your objectives: Documenting your objectives can enhance their concreteness and assist in maintaining your accountability. Maintain the visibility of your objectives by placing them in prominent locations, such as a well-organized planner or a thoughtfully designed vision board, and consistently review them to monitor and gauge your advancements.

6. Acknowledge your accomplishments: Ultimately, acknowledge the progress you have made in pursuit of your objectives. Recognize your accomplishments, regardless of their magnitude, and employ them as a source of inspiration to continue striving for your overarching aspirations.

To summarize, establishing meaningful objectives is a crucial element of proficient time allocation. By adhering to these prescribed procedures, you can establish a foundation for success and attain your envisioned results.

Fewer Distractions From One's Coworkers Overall

In the workplace, one of the most significant sources of distraction is one's coworkers. Someone popping by to drop something off or even just passing by might eat up a significant portion of your day, regardless of whether you work in a cubicle or have your own office. It could seem like a good idea to take a break and just have some fun, but if you do so, you will very likely end up falling behind on the task that you are currently working on. This does not occur when you are working from home, which enables you to continue working without losing your concentration. Even if coworkers at your place of employment try to communicate with you using electronic mail or a message service, you are not required to react right away. If, on the other hand, they are directly in front of you at the office, it will be difficult for you to avoid them.

More time for you to spend on yourself
You will rapidly come to the realisation that, as a result of working from home, you end up having more time for yourself. Because you are not obligated to get up early, you have the option of getting additional sleep or making use of this time to engage in physical activity. You won't have to worry about being in a hurry during your lunch break, so you can put that time towards getting some housework done instead. People who were quarantined at home during the epidemic took up hobbies like gardening, baking, and cooking because they had extra time on their hands. All of this adds to a healthy work-life balance, which can be hugely beneficial to one's overall health. As a consequence, all of this leads to improved performance at work as a result of a more well-rounded lifestyle.

These are only some of the most important aspects that contribute to an increase in productivity when working from home. They are all centred around gaining more free time so that you can work and live the manner you want for yourself. Although this is incredibly exciting news, it is important to note that not everyone has the same experience when they work from home. It is my mission to reassure you that experiencing difficulties while working from home is normal and acceptable. It is natural to experience some initial difficulty in maintaining your previous level of productivity when making this move because it is not always an easy process. I have been in your shoes, and dealing with similar challenges is one of the primary motivations for why I decided to write this book. Working from the comfort of your own home is something that is an option for you. You just need to figure out why you are having so much trouble, and after that, you will be able to take the required actions to better your circumstances.

12 Parenting Hacks

Having access to effective parenting hacks is incredibly important for single moms as they navigate the challenges of raising their kids solo.

Single moms often carry a heavy load of responsibilities, and the hacks listed in this chapter can provide them with valuable guidance and shortcuts to ensure their children's well-being and development.

Whether it's tips on managing behavior, organizing schedules, or fostering educational activities, these hacks can be a lifesaver. They help single moms optimize their limited time and resources, fostering a positive and nurturing environment for their children.

By implementing these parenting hacks, single moms can gain more confidence in their abilities and create a stable, loving, and supportive home for their children, ultimately setting their children up for success in life.

It doesn't have to be all or nothing.

Many single-moms grapple with feelings of inadequacy because they can't provide everything they desire for their children. However, you must come to realize that it doesn't have to be an all-or-nothing scenario. As a single mom, you often tend to be overly critical of yourself, forgetting that every effort counts, no matter how small.

It's crucial to acknowledge that every action, no matter how modest, contributes to positivity in your children's lives. Instead of dwelling on what you can't do, focus on what you can. For instance, while you might not have time to volunteer regularly in your kid's classrooms, you can take pride in chaperoning a field trip once or twice a year. This demonstrates that even occasional efforts are noteworthy and impactful.

Single parenting often comes with financial, time, and energy constraints. It's essential to come to terms with the reality that you can't provide everything your children may desire. Acknowledge your limitations and understand that they don't diminish your dedication as a mother.

One of the key aspects of adopting an "It doesn't have to be all or nothing" mindset is giving yourself credit for your efforts. Whether it's organizing a special family activity, attending a school event, or simply being there to listen to your children, these gestures are valuable and deserve recognition.

Rather than spreading yourself thin by attempting to provide everything, prioritize the quality of the experiences you can offer. While you may not be able to enroll your children in all the lessons or extracurricular activities they desire, focus on the meaningful moments you can create together.

Single parenting teaches you to appreciate the value of what you can provide. While you may not be able to host lavish parties, endless playdates, or frequent vacations, you can focus on the joy you can bring into your children's lives throughout gestures and shared experiences.

Single parenting often prompts feelings of guilt and inadequacy due to the inability to fulfill every desire or need. However, recognizing that it doesn't have to be an all-or-nothing endeavor empowers you to appreciate the value of your efforts, no matter how limited they may be.

By giving yourself credit for what you can do and prioritizing meaningful moments over quantity, you can provide your children with a rich and fulfilling upbringing, even within the confines of your resources and circumstances.

Chapter 3: Pomodoro Technique

Introduction to the Pomodoro Technique

In a world filled with constant distractions, staying focused and productive can be a real challenge. This is where the Pomodoro Technique comes into play, a time management strategy that aims to help individuals improve their ability to stay focused and increase productivity, turning time into an ally instead of an enemy.

The Pomodoro technique was developed by Francesco Cirillo in the late 1980s. It is named for the tomato-shaped kitchen timer, or "pomodoro" in Italian, that Cirillo used during his college years. This strategy is based on the idea that frequent breaks can improve mental alertness and concentration.

The technique divides the work into blocks of time, usually 25 minutes, separated by short rest intervals, which are five minutes. These intervals are known as "pomodoros." After completing four pomodoros, it is recommended to take a longer break, 15 to 30 minutes. The intention of this structure is to provide adequate time to focus intensely on a task, with breaks that help maintain energy and concentration over time, avoiding burnout.

The appeal of the Pomodoro technique lies in its simplicity. You don't need any specialized equipment, just a timer and a task to perform. It is also flexible and can be tailored to individual needs, adjusting the length of the pomodoros and breaks to optimize personal productivity.

Furthermore, this technique not only helps improve productivity, but is also effective in promoting greater awareness of how time is used. By dividing work into specific time segments, one can begin to recognize how long it actually takes to complete certain tasks. This can help improve time planning and reduce stress associated with always feeling like you have too much to do and too little time to do it.

However, while the Pomodoro technique can be extremely useful, it is not the perfect solution for everyone or for every task. It requires a commitment to time structure and doesn't work as well with tasks that require long periods of uninterrupted concentration. However, for many people, the Pomodoro technique can be an incredibly effective time management tool, providing the necessary structure to help maintain focus and increase productivity.

The Pomodoro Technique is a time management strategy that focuses on segmenting work into specific time intervals, interspersed with breaks. It provides a structured framework to improve concentration and productivity, while promoting a greater awareness of how time is spent.

Misconceptions That Are Widespread Debunked

The ability to effectively manage one's time is an essential one; yet, it is essential to differentiate between useful practises and widespread fallacies, which can actually impair one's productivity.

It is more efficient to multitask: A lot of people are under the impression that they may increase their level of productivity by juggling many responsibilities at once. In practise, attempting to multitask frequently results in decreased efficiency as well as lower quality work. This can lead to blunders as well as an increase in tension because it divides your concentration. In most cases, the most productive approach is to concentrate on completing one task at a time.

Activity Levels Correlate to Levels of Productivity: Some people believe that having a full schedule is synonymous with being productive. However, maintaining a high level of activity without advancing towards the completion of any significant goals might be harmful. It is crucial to prioritise jobs not only for the purpose of filling your schedule, but rather on the basis of their importance and value.

More Hours Worked Equals Greater Productivity: The idea that putting in more hours at work would result in higher levels of productivity is a widespread fallacy. In point of fact, working too hard might result in burnout, which in turn can lead to diminished creativity and efficiency. The quantity of hours put in is less important than one's ability to effectively manage their time and the quality of their job.

The Importance of Everything Is the Same: The importance of each and every job is not the same. The misconception that you have to give equal weight to all of your responsibilities can result in inefficient time management on your part. Use methods instead, such as the Eisenhower Matrix (which will be discussed in a later chapter), to prioritise jobs according to their level of importance and level of urgency.

It Is Possible to "Catch Up" on Sleep You've Missed A lot of individuals have the misconception that they may sacrifice sleep in order to become more productive and then "catch up" on sleep they've missed at a later time. This is a harmful fallacy because prolonged sleep deprivation can lead to health concerns, impaired cognitive function, and overall lower productivity. However, this belief has persisted for a long time.

The pursuit of perfection increases productivity: Trying to achieve perfection in everything you do can cause you to waste time and add unnecessary stress to your life. Even though having high standards is a commendable trait, there is a limit beyond which perfectionism stops being effective. It is frequently more productive to strive for excellence and then move on to the next undertaking.

You Are Required to Reply Instantaneously: Some people have the impression that they have an obligation to instantly answer to every email, message, or request that is sent to them. This ongoing reactivity can make it difficult for you to concentrate and get tasks done. An technique that can be more efficient is to schedule particular times to check and respond to communications at predetermined intervals.

Being Helpful Means Constantly Responding "Yes" to Every Request: It's good to be helpful, but if you say "yes" to every request or obligation, you run the risk of becoming overcommitted and losing effectiveness. The ability to master the art of the polite but firm "no" when the situation calls for it is fundamental to effective time management.

It is a Complete Waste of Time to Plan: Some individuals are of the opinion that planning and organising their responsibilities takes up an excessive amount of time, and that they should instead jump right into their work. On the other hand, planning ahead and organising your tasks according to their importance can help you get more done in less time by improving the quality of your work.

There is No Way to Avoid Putting Things Off: Procrastination is seen by many people as either a natural and necessary component of the creative process or as a necessary but undesirable aspect of the process. Even if procrastination could rear its head every once in a while, it is critical to acknowledge that it is a barrier to productivity and work on devising methods to overcome it.

Individuals may improve their productivity, experience less stress, and strike a better balance between their professional and personal lives by debunking the myths around time management and adopting more efficient practises.

Cultivating A Mentality Of Growth And Expansion

It is impossible to exaggerate how important it is to be able to adjust to new circumstances and continue to educate oneself in order to thrive in a world that is always shifting and becoming more complex. We go deep into the world of a growth mindset throughout the pages of this chapter. A growth mindset is a powerful mental framework that not only reveres the process of learning but also excitedly embraces challenges and firmly defends the potency of self-improvement. You are about to embark on a trip that has the potential to catapult you into the realm of unrelenting advancement. In this realm, you will make use of your innate strengths to overcome challenges and realise incredible victories.

What It Means to Have a "Growth Mindset"

The essence of a mindset that lives on development and enlightenment is encapsulated at the very heart of what it is to have a growth mindset. It stands in direct contrast to the fixed mindset, which is the belief that one's talents and abilities are unchangeable characteristics that cannot be developed further. A growth mindset, on the other hand, considers one's talents and abilities to be fluid things that are capable of undergoing development and improvement as a result of focused work, tenacity, and further education.

The Value of Being Willing to Face Obstacles

Imagine a situation in which obstacles are not roadblocks but rather stepping stones, where setbacks become opportunities, and where failures serve as launchpads for growth; this is the kind of world we are imagining. This shift in mentality is the defining characteristic of taking on challenges with a view towards personal development. As you continue along this road, you will be able to observe how the difficulties that you formerly found intimidating transform into opportunities for growth. In the same way that a blade is forged by a blacksmith by subjecting it to great heat and pressure, you too may create your personality, abilities, and capacities by putting yourself in situations that force you to overcome obstacles.

Learning That Lasts a Lifetime: A Shining Example

Learning should be viewed as a process that continues throughout one's life, rather than as a discrete event. You can maintain your adaptability in the face of shifting conditions by placing a high value on and actively pursuing ongoing learning. Your commitment to education guarantees that you won't fall behind the unstoppable onslaught of time, the rapid growth of technology, and the morphing of prevailing paradigms. Your dedication to continual learning gives you the tools you need to succeed in a world that is constantly changing, whether that means becoming an expert in emerging technologies or maintaining familiarity with the latest developments in your field.

Converting Obstacles into Launchpads for Future Success

Every victory has its roots planted firmly in the rich ground of adversity and dogged determination. A growth mindset recognises that mistakes and failures are natural and necessary parts of the learning process. An individual who is focused on growth is one who, in the face of challenges, is able to grow, adapt, and ultimately prevail over those challenges. You may empower yourself to learn from your mistakes and develop an unwavering spirit of resilience by viewing your setbacks as stepping stones rather than stumbling obstacles.

Get ready to break through barriers and realise your full potential as you begin this chapter's investigation of developing a growth mindset. You will learn how to do both of these things. You will discover a greater understanding of your capacity to change, adapt, and rise above the challenges that lie ahead of you through the experiences of others who have adopted this attitude, the practical techniques presented, and the transforming practises emphasised. Therefore, embark on this path of growth, and allow the transformation to start when you do.

Developing An Individualised Timetable While Creating An Effective Time Management System

In the beginning...

Developing a timetable that is unique to your needs is an essential step on the path to better time management. This chapter looks into the process of building a time management system that is suited to the specific requirements, preferences, and objectives of the individual reader. The readers are able to improve their daily routines, raise their levels of productivity, and achieve a more harmonious balance between their professional and personal hobbies if they create a tailored timetable for themselves.

Recognizing the Importance of Having a Tailored Timetable

A time management strategy that treats every person the same and ignores their particular ities and the specifics of their lives is not effective. This section examines the significance of developing one's own unique schedule and the ways in which doing so enables one to make the most of their available time and resources. The reader will be able to construct a schedule that is congruent with their lifestyle and improves their overall well-being if they take the time to learn their individual patterns, preferences, and priorities.

Adaptation to Personal Rhythms refers to the process of designing a schedule that is in sync with one's natural energy levels and peaks in terms of productivity.

Increasing one's productivity involves determining the best times to complete various chores in order to improve one's effectiveness and output.

Taking Care of Personal Obligations Incorporating personal obligations, such as spending time with one's family and participating in hobbies, into one's calendar.

A tailored timetable minimizes the amount of time spent making decisions, which in turn reduces stress and a sense of being overwhelmed.

Improving Work-Life Balance is striking a healthy balance between one's professional responsibilities and one's personal hobbies by strategically allocating one's time.

Before developing a tailored plan, it is necessary to do an analysis of the ways in which time is presently being spent, as this is the first step in the process. In this section, we will discuss methods for keeping track of time, determining where time is being wasted, and recognizing patterns of productivity and distraction. The readers will be able to find areas in which they could improve their daily routines by receiving insights into how they already use their time.

Keeping a clear record of daily activities and how time is spent is an essential component of time tracking.

Reviewing time logs in order to search for patterns, activities that are time wasters, and routines that are counterproductive.

Identifying tasks that take up an inordinate amount of time without providing significant rewards is one aspect of recognizing time sinks.

Assessing Productivity Patterns involves identifying peak productive hours as well as times of diminished focus on the task at hand.

Putting Essential Tasks in Their Proper Priority entails locating high-priority endeavors that need your undivided attention.

Developing a Plan for the Management of Time:

This section discusses the step-by-step process of building a tailored time management system, beginning with a thorough comprehension of how time is currently being used. The reader will gain an understanding of how to design a timetable that is both flexible and structured, and which takes into account their individual requirements and objectives. In order to foster better overall health, we will talk about how to strike a healthy balance between one's professional life, one's personal life, and one's own self-care.

Defining consistent routines for morning, work hours, and evening is an important step in the process of establishing core daily routines.

Setting Aside precise Amounts of Time For High-Priority Tasks Setting aside precise amounts of time for important endeavors and objectives is referred to as "blocking" time.

Including "Buffer Time," also known as "Leaving Room for Unexpected Tasks," "Taking Breaks," and "Relaxing,"

Having the ability to be flexible and adaptable means developing a timetable that can be modified to account for shifting priorities and other commitments.

Putting Yourself First: Putting your own health and well-being first by making it a priority to schedule time for self-care activities.

Addressing Personal and Professional Goals: Balancing short-term and long-term goals in the schedule.

Implementing ways to remove time-wasting activities and distractions is an important step in the process of minimizing time wasters.

How To Take Charge Of Your Day By Creating An Efficient To-Do List

The to-do list opens off with the activities from the day before. Before you leave the office for the day, you should make an effort to scribble down a rough draft of the work you need to do or have left for the following day. This will be utilized for the purpose of filling out the activities on tomorrow's to-do list without wasting time on hard thinking or remembering what those duties are and how much work was left over from the previous day.

The following morning, the most productive thing you could do would be to create a rough to-do list. It can include any things that were not completed from the previous day's to-do list as well as anything else that comes to mind at that particular instant. Let there be as many flaws as possible in it. When we make our morning to-do list, we always put a lot of thought into it, and we give a lot of consideration to whether or not something was forgotten or whether or not we are able to remember it. The truth is that as the day progresses, we have a tendency to remember items that we might have overlooked while making the to-do list in the morning. This is because as we continue to complete tasks, our memories tend to refresh.

Therefore, the things that need to be done list ought to be malleable, living, ever-shifting, and founded on the requirements of the moment; it ought to be updated, and it ought to direct us toward the tasks that we need to complete during the day.

As soon as the rough draft is finished, we begin adding the activities one at a time to the list of things to do for the fair, putting them in the order of priority and grouping comparable jobs together if it is practicable to do so.

So, what should be contained within it? It does not matter whether the activities and jobs are interesting or mundane as long as they are included. It is not appropriate to include any aims or objectives. Desired results are referred to as goals and objectives, yet in many instances, they cannot be pinned down to a single day. Therefore, if it is anything along the lines of "work towards being the highest sales making department," it is quite ambiguous and rather reassuring, which allows one to avoid working really toward it. Instead, write "work for contacting 10 prospective customers" and "closing more than 3 sales today." These are more actionable goals. It is possible to further dissect it by identifying a potential consumer by name and the amount of time we have to spend communicating or interacting with them.

It's possible for a task or activity to be both mundane and essential to your job at the same time. It's possible that completing such chores will take a significant amount of time. It will be of use to us in determining how much time we actually have available for carrying out all of these activities. There should consistently be at least one or two activities available that add both excitement and significance to the day. Those are the kinds of activities that hold significant importance for either your professional advancement or your own personal growth. They will assist you in jumping on to finish the to-do list with enthusiasm so that you can acquire that feeling of fulfillment or achievement at the end of the day. It will energize you to put in the effort necessary to finish the to-do list.

Therefore, before we look at an example of a to-do list, let's go over some of the helpful tips that may be used when building a list:

• Before the end of the day, jot down a rough draft of the to-do list for the following day. Then, at the beginning of the following day, revise and update the list while also adding new items to it. The items on a to-do list may shift about a little bit as the day progresses. If the adjustment is significant, you will need to create a new list by consulting the comprehensive view of your weekly schedule that you have.

- To the best of your ability, prioritize the activities you have to complete and arrange your duties accordingly. If any unimportant work that takes less time can be batched along with some vital jobs, then you can club it together; however, if it takes a significant amount of time, then you will need to choose according to the priority list. In the following chapter, titled "The Power of Prioritization," we will go over the various methods for prioritization in further detail.

Even if you use tactics for prioritization, you can discover that a number of jobs have to be completed at a specific time, and that time should be set in stone. If you are scheduled to meet with someone from another department in the afternoon, you will have to resolve this issue during that specific window of time only. As a result, chores of this nature, where earlier appointments or scheduling has already been completed, are the ones that should be fixed first.

According to the priority of each activity, which will be discussed in greater depth in the following chapter titled "The Power of Prioritization," all other activities will either be rescheduled or reorganized so that they may fit around the duties that have already been set in stone.

• Limit your to-do list to no more than five to eight items at a time:

The question is, how many items should a list of things to do contain? It is stated that the average human being is capable of maintaining a high level of concentration for 25 to 35 minutes at a time. Therefore, if we take roughly three hours before lunch and three hours after lunch, the maximum number of assignments would be somewhere between ten and twelve. To reiterate, we do not do every activity within the allotted 35 minutes. Or, not all tasks require more than half an hour to complete. The amount of time required for each job on your to-do list is the primary factor that determines the number of tasks that need to be completed.

Take, for instance: An HR executive may need a whole day to complete the process of distributing helmets inside the factory to a workforce of 1,000 individuals; this operation may involve driving a moving vehicle stocked with helmets to each department and distributing them there.

Strategies For Increasing One's Own Productivity

The Method of the Pomodoro Timer
The Pomodoro Technique is a well-known approach for managing one's time that entails dividing up one's workday into focused intervals of a usual length of 25 minutes, which are then followed by a brief rest of 5 minutes. After completing four Pomodoro intervals, you should reward yourself with a lengthier respite, lasting between 15 and 30 minutes. Concentration may be maintained with the help of this strategy, which also helps prevent burnout. It is especially useful for activities that call for a high level of concentration.

Getting Rid of the Practice of Multitasking
The widespread idea that multitasking is an effective method of time management

couldn't be further from the truth. In point of fact, it frequently lowers productivity and raises the rate of errors. Concentrate on doing one activity at a time rather than trying to juggle numerous responsibilities at once. It is much more probable that you will finish a task successfully and precisely if you give it your undivided attention when you work on it.

The Golden Rule of Two Minutes

The Two-Minute Rule is a straightforward but effective piece of advice. If a task can be finished in two minutes or less, you should start working on it right away. Tasks such as submitting a document, returning a phone call, or responding to quick emails are examples of the types of activities that frequently fall into this category. You may prevent minor responsibilities from stacking up and becoming more time-consuming in the future if you take care of them as soon as they arise.

Establishing Crystal-Clear Objectives And Priorities

Establishing What Your Goals Are

Having well-defined objectives is the first step toward efficient time management. Before you can effectively manage your time, you need to have a clear idea of the goals you want to accomplish with it. The formulation of goals that are specific, measurable, achievable, relevant, and time-bound are referred to as SMART goals. It is vital to develop SMART goals in order to advance in one's profession, complete a project, or improve one's work-life balance.

A good example of a SMART goal would be "Increase my weekly sales by 15% within the next three months by implementing a new sales strategy." This would be more specific than a goal such as "Improve work performance," which is too general.

The Eisenhower Reconstruction Matrix

The Eisenhower Matrix is a useful tool for determining priorities since it divides work into four different quadrants, each of which corresponds to a different level of importance and urgency:

These responsibilities demand that you give them your full attention right away, and they are quite important.

Important but Not Urgent: These activities are important, but they do not need to be completed immediately because they can be postponed.

Not Important but Urgent: These responsibilities may appear to be pressing, but they often contribute less to long-term goals.

Not Urgent and Not Important: The completion of these jobs is a waste of time and need to be reduced or avoided entirely.

By classifying your responsibilities using this matrix, you will be able to zero in on what genuinely matters and steer clear of becoming mired down by things that are less significant.

Establishing Crystal-Clear Objectives And Priorities

Now that we have a firm grasp on the fundamentals of time management, we are in a position to move on to more specific objectives. Everyone has visions of the person they eventually aspire to become. Daydreaming is not the same as actually being that person since being that person requires having clear goals. This chapter will discuss two different topics. Introspection is one of these methods. You'll have the opportunity to reflect on yourself and address questions like, "What do I want to achieve at work?" and "What do I want my life to look like?"

In the second part of this guide, we'll discuss some strategies that will help you move closer to achieving your goals.

This will provide you with a more methodical approach as opposed to just making educated guesses. It turns out that if you get used to it, it's also much simpler than making educated guesses! Consequently, let's begin by investigating why setting goals is important in the first place.

Identifying One's Own Personal and Professional Objectives

It is essential to your ability to effectively manage your time that you correctly identify the objectives you wish to work towards. The explanation for this is rather straightforward: people who are good at managing their time are aware of the aspects of their lives in which they excel and where those strengths combine with feelings of satisfaction. In a nutshell, they spend more time focusing on the things that bring them joy. This is the fundamental idea that underpins Dr.Verkamp's proposal for a 168-hour work week. She refers to these as core competences, and her support for them has led her to the conclusion that it is appropriate to relocate and change careers. That is, of course, assuming the reader is able to concentrate on their own specialization and can manage such a significant adjustment. However, making such recommendations is outside the scope of my job responsibilities.

To avoid getting into too much detail, however, goals have a significant influence on how we behave. Writing an essay for the sake of writing an essay is not the same as writing an essay because you believe it will make you a better writer. There is a discernible difference between the two. In their study on productivity, conducted in 1974, Latham and Kinne came to the following conclusion: "Goal setting leads to a significant increase in the productivity of the group as well as the individual." This study served as a prime example of this concept. They also discovered that delegating goals to team leaders had an effect that was more significant and more evenly distributed. Since then, a significant amount of time has passed. These days, conventional approaches for goal planning are developed bearing in mind both personnel and the projects they are working on. Among these approaches, the SMART Goals framework stands out as one that is very pertinent to the work we are doing.

If you've spent more than a week working in an office, the acronym SMART is presumably already familiar to you in some capacity. You come from a project management background, and this is one of the tools that you rely on the most. According to findings from a study that was conducted by Cothran and Wysocki in 2005, "It is important that goals meet specific criteria that can be used to easily assess them." Utilizing the acronym "SMART" as a criterion for success in this endeavor is one approach that might be taken. In point of fact, this instrument provides us with a foundation upon which we can develop both our personal and professional objectives. If all of the conditions are satisfied, then we ought to acknowledge that they are valid. In turn, this helps us have well-defined goals that we can focus on, which is a huge benefit. Specific, Measurable, Achievable, Relevant, and Time-Bound are the components that make up the acronym SMART.

Being specific relates to the manner in which we define our objective. We ought to aim for a specific target while also making it simple to articulate to other people. As we are formulating a particular objective, we ought to decide where, when, how, and with whom we will accomplish it.

Objectives that are measurable enable progress to be monitored. When we look back on it, we can easily claim that roughly 30 percent of the work for it is done. Increasing the quantifiability of an aim can be accomplished in a straightforward manner by adding milestones. To guarantee that we can measure our progress toward our objective, it is helpful to know what factors influence whether or not it has been accomplished.

Although it may sound restrictive, achievable is actually much more open-ended than you might at first imagine. Our objective need to be an attainable target, just like its namesake says, so that we may successfully complete it. A aim such as opening a restaurant on one of Jupiter's moons, for instance, would not fulfill the requirements of the criterion. In spite of this, we must not be afraid of obstacles. The complexity of a goal should be proportional to its importance. It is also essential that you leave some wiggle room for the situation to evolve. There will be times when circumstances arise that make it difficult to achieve a particular objective. It is a terrific approach to spare yourself some headaches if you have the ability to adjust just a single parameter rather than the entire notion.

The degree to which these goals match with larger goals is directly related to their level of relevance. For instance, efforts within a corporation ought to be in agreement with the organization's particular core values and ought to continue to be compatible with preceding actions. The pursuit of our individual goals shouldn't lead us to operate in a manner that is inconsistent with who we are. In a phrase: just be yourself!

Last but not least, we need to discuss what it means for goals to have a time limit. They begin at a predetermined point and must be completed before the allotted time. There would be no use in trying to be more productive or manage time if they didn't have it; it would be pointless. The imposition of constraints inevitably results in optimization.

Consider your options for a while before making a decision about where you wish to go. The goals that you have set for yourself to achieve your dreams. The folks whose identities are still a mystery to you but whom you can't wait to get to know. They may be professional or personal, but it would be best if they were a combination of the two. After you are finished, you can list them. Take note of the category that each of these falls within. I would like for you to examine these needs and assess whether or not they meet the prerequisites that have been outlined. If they do, that would be wonderful! You are currently working toward some long-term goals that you have set. On the other hand, it is more likely that they forgot one or two of the components. That is not in the least bit problematic. Why don't you attempt to fill in the blanks as a starting point for where to go from here?

I'll illustrate this point with a dream I've had for a very long time. My goal has always been to start an indoor garden so that I can always have access to fresh herbs and vegetables. Even if I've read a few books on growing tomatoes and lettuce, there are still a few additional plants whose cultivation I need to learn more about. In addition to that, I need to construct the area, prepare the garden, and plant the seeds for the initial crop. My goal has been clear and easy to measure up to this point. Knowing myself, I can complete the task in a reasonable amount of time each day, which comes to approximately an hour. Taking into consideration whether it goes against my beliefs or interferes with the progress of other projects, we are in the clear. As of late, I've been wrapping up a number of side projects, which means I'll have ample amounts of free time. As a result, we have arrived at the conclusion that it is pertinent. Because of the potential importance of accountability, it is imperative that I establish a time limit for when it will be operational. In light of this, I will speculate that the undertaking will be finished prior to the year 2023 coming to a close. We have been successful in establishing a time limit, and in addition to that, we have transformed a wishful thinking into a SMART goal.

It's not unheard of to feel as though our jobs and our personal lives are tugging us in completely different directions. This is not the inevitable state of affairs. The greatest method to experience less of a divide between your job and who you are as a person is to lessen the significance of this distinction. This does not imply that John's personal life should be dominated by numbers and precise calculations simply because he works in accounting; on the contrary, this is not the case. Instead, the focus should be on ensuring that different objectives do not compete with one another. If John, following our example, wants to advance his career within the next year and also has the objective of becoming a vigilante during the evenings, both of these ambitions will fight for his time. As a result, it is highly improbable that John will make significant progress toward either goal.

Instead, keep the R in SMART front and center in your mind. Keeping up with current events and remaining relevant gives us the opportunity to be whoever we want to be. If we do not keep it in mind, we may experience the opposite effect, which is feeling disjointed and tight. Prioritization will be discussed in a manner not dissimilar to that of significance. Let's find out which of our goals should take up the most of our time now that we've set a couple of them.

Prioritization, As Well As The Establishment Of Goals

Establishing One's Goals and Ordering One's Concerns in Order to Realize One's Potential

In a world that is always humming with distractions and conflicting demands on our time, the ability to set clear, relevant aims and efficiently prioritize work is akin to having a superpower. Setting clear, relevant targets and efficiently prioritizing work is like having a superpower. It is the key to unlocking your full potential and achieving the things that are most important to you. This chapter will not only instruct you on how to set reasonable goals for yourself. These two ideas, when taken together, will cause a shift in the way you think about the activities and goals you have set for yourself.

A Method for Establishing Wise Objectives

"An aim without a strategy is just a wish,"

Have you ever set a goal for yourself at the beginning of the year, only to abandon it by February? In that case, you are not the only one. Many people, in the absence of a clearly articulated plan, set nebulous, unachievable goals for themselves that are difficult to achieve. In a scenario like this one, you can make use of smart objectives.

One of a kind: Your purpose must to be crystal clear and unequivocally stated. It ought to be obvious what it is that I want to achieve by reading it. Why is it important to understand this? Who else is going to be there? Where is it going to take place exactly? What kinds of limitations are there?

Having a goal that is both measurable and attainable makes it easier to track your progress. It addresses questions such as, "How will I know when it is finished?" and "What are the possible outcomes?" What are some observable and quantifiable indicators of success?

Your target ought to be realizable, but at the same time, it ought to stretch your capacities. It is essential to find a happy medium while setting goals for oneself, ensuring that they are challenging but not insurmountable at the same time.

To the point: Is your ambition in line with the wider goals and fundamental ideas that guide your organization? It is essential that it is congruent with your larger objectives and that it reflects your sense of mission.

Restricted in Time: A goal that does not have a time limit attached to it is just a wish. You may assist people feel motivated and dedicated to your goal by providing them with a deadline.

For the purpose of demonstrating how the smart framework functions, let's take a common goal: "I want to lose weight."

I want to run more so that I can lose 15 pounds and improve my cardiovascular fitness, and I want to do both by increasing the amount that I run.

Easily Measured: "Using a fitness app, I'll keep tabs on my weight and running progress."

The possibility: "I'll begin with a doable plan, seeking the advice of a fitness professional as necessary."

Have you noticed the way in which this shrewd purpose provides direction and clarity? It clarifies a general goal and turns it into a detailed plan of action.

It is imperative that you read this: These tasks usually include time-sensitive concerns that need for immediate attention from the employee. Managing an emergency medical condition or meeting a stringent professional deadline are two examples of this. These are the most important things for you to focus on.

But even though they don't have a hard and fast end date, these tasks are absolutely necessary to the accomplishment of your long-term goals. Some of them include physical activity, cultivating relationships, and expanding one's skill set. This should be a top focus if you want to be successful over the long term.

The activities in this quadrant may appear to be time-sensitive, but they won't really move you closer to achieving your goals. They usually involve time-wasting activities such as meaningless phone calls or meetings. Determine several methods to cut down on these distractions.

In the area of "Not Urgent" and "Not Important," you can find activities that are a waste of time as well as endeavors that do not support your goals or ideals. This involves watching multiple hours of television at once and wasting time on social media. Cut back on or eliminate as much of these as you can from your life.

When you make the essential but less pressing responsibilities your top priority, magic happens. These are the deeds that have a big impact on your life and move you one step closer to accomplishing the goals you have set for yourself over the long run. On the other hand, in the frenzy of dealing with day-to-day crises, they are frequently overlooked.

Wellness and Physical Exercise: A healthy lifestyle, including regular exercise, as well as preventative medical care, can assist in lowering the risk of future health problems.

Investments in Your Personal Development Developing new skills, reading, and taking time to reflect on how you've behaved are all valuable ways to make personal development investments.

Relationships: Cultivating healthy relationships with one's family, friends, and coworkers can lead to the formation of close bonds and an increase in overall life satisfaction.

Progression in One's Career Advancing one's career can be accomplished through the cultivation of networks, the execution of strategic plans, and the acquisition of new skills.

Acquire Command Of Your Own Time.

Setting Priorities for Work

It is highly desired to be able to select and execute activities in the order of importance, and certain types of businesses present a greater challenge in this regard than others.

In order to select tasks, you need to be aware of the maximum number of responsibilities and projects that are available. In order to accomplish this, each planning session needs to include the creation of a list.

You Absolutely Need to Keep a List!

Make a list of all of your obligations, rate them, and then make another list of them in order. After then, you can put them on your schedule. After assigning ratings to all of the activities and projects, proceed to prioritize by using the following additional filters:

• Consider the repercussions that would result from eliminating the task. – Performing this exercise will frequently result in the elimination of some duties that are unnecessary.

• Determine if each activity should be carried out during the primary or secondary time period.

• Identify the individuals whose lives will be changed by the activity. Now Cut Down on Your List.

The majority of us will need to lighten our burden until we figure out how to clone ourselves so that we can effectively be in more than one location at once.

Before you start assigning priorities, think about the following criteria for eliminating tasks:

Does It Make Sense to Carry Out This Task or Project?

You should make it a requirement that every task you complete must first meet this standard.

You have things that you want to accomplish, priorities, and goals. Does each and every task contribute in some way to your overall goal? Make an educated guess as to how much time will be required to complete each work, and then consider how you might spend that time if the task were to be scrapped. Every action you take should contribute in some manner to achieving your goals, even if this isn't always achievable.

Why is the Task Needed So Quickly?

Although having a sense of urgency should be a mindset for business, that sense of urgency should also be relentlessly questioned. Is the urgency a result of trying to appease another person? Why is there such a sense of rushing now? There have been a lot of mistakes that have led to serious circumstances. Determining the reason for the urgency can lead to the elimination or postponement of a work, as well as the development of preventative measures against interruptions and errors.

There are some tasks that appear to be really urgent but actually aren't. There is a possibility that customers are making requests that are not essential.

Make sure you ask each of the concerned parties.

The Qualifying Event for the Delegation

Do you consider yourself to be the only person capable of completing the task? There will be occasions when you are, but there will also be times when someone else can perform in your place. To free up more time in your schedule, you should delegate everything that can be.

In What Other Ways Could the Task Be Carried Out?

Are you making use of modern technology?

Would a phone call suffice in place of an in-person appointment?

The use of conference calling can eliminate the need to travel, which results in significant time savings.

Would you be able to email rather than call?

You are free to check your email whenever and however you like.

In comparison to the live telephone chat, you will have more time to carefully clarify your thoughts. When we leave voicemails for other people, we not only waste time but also risk losing sales. Email puts an end to the game of phone tag.

Is It Possible to Break Down the Task?

Are there parts of the work that could be deleted, postponed, or delegated to another person?

What are the Repercussions of Not Completing a Task?

There are a great number of tasks that arise throughout the day that are not really worth the time it takes to do them. When thinking about whether or not to cancel an assignment, applying the dollar figure is another way to estimate the value of the task.

1- An Overview of Time Management Strategies for Entrepreneurs

Cognizance of the Significance of Delegation and Team Administration

Effectively managing one's time is an essential factor in running a successful enterprise. The effective management and appropriate allocation of valuable resources can greatly determine the success or failure of any institution. The extensive range of responsibilities faced by a business proprietor includes the administration of financial matters, the execution of marketing initiatives, the oversight of day-to-day operations, and the implementation of strategic decisions. In light of the numerous responsibilities one must manage, it is crucial to effectively structure one's schedule to prioritize specific tasks and communicate responsibilities efficiently. To accomplish this prioritization, the effective management of tasks can be facilitated through the practice of delegating responsibilities to colleagues or subordinates.

In this section, we will explore the significance of allocating and arranging time for entrepreneurs. Moreover, we will elaborate on how the practice of delegation and implementation of management strategies can enhance productivity, while facilitating the attainment of one's business objectives.

The Significance of Time Management for Entrepreneurial Leaders

There are few things as invaluable to an entrepreneur as time. Through the effective utilization of time, individuals can optimize their limited resources and direct their focus towards tasks of utmost significance. As a result, this contributes to the enhanced achievement of objectives by maximizing the utilization of the available time.

Insufficient allocation of priorities and ineffective scheduling can lead to the failure of meeting deadlines, the production of work of substandard quality, and diminished efficiency. These deficiencies have noteworthy implications for your company's financial position as they decrease sources of income. Conversely, proficient time allocation can assist you in:

To enhance your efficiency, it is imperative that you prioritize the tasks of utmost significance and allocate appropriate attention to them.

Identify and analyze areas where time can be conserved and processes can be optimized to enhance operational efficiency.

Assign responsibilities to members of your team, thus enabling yourself to allocate more time towards the contemplation and implementation of strategic choices.

By alleviating the causes of stress and fatigue, you can improve your mental well-being and overall state of health.

Establishing Goals

A

As one embarks on the journey of personal development, it becomes evident that establishing clearly defined objectives acts as a definitive navigational instrument for one's advancement. Objectives provide guidance, impetus, and a profound sense of meaning. Within this chapter, we will thoroughly examine the art and science behind effective goal-setting, specifically focusing on the establishment of SMART goals. SMART goals are characterized by their specificity, measurability, achievability, relevance, and time-bound nature. By attaining mastery in this skill, you will establish the groundwork for a prosperous trajectory towards personal growth and development.

The Importance of Establishing Objectives:

Goal setting transcends mere procedural tasks or exercises; it embodies a metamorphic process that confers upon you the ability to...

● Establish Your Objective; Objectives provide clarity to your vision and emphasize your projected destination in the forthcoming future.

- Provide Motivation; They. Take proactive measures in response to obstacles.

- Monitor Progress; Objectives serve as yardsticks for assessing your development.

- Enhance Self-Assurance: The realization of goals fortifies one's self-esteem and bolsters faith in one's capabilities.

- Improve Concentration: Objectives aid in the effective allocation of resources and prioritization of efforts.

However, not all objectives possess equivalent significance. In order to enhance their efficacy, we depend on the utilization of the SMART framework.

Precision: The Significance of Being \\\'SMART\\\'

One characteristic of an effective goal is its precise and unambiguous nature, leaving no room for confusion or misinterpretation. It is imperative that it addresses the inquiries of 'what,' 'why,' and 'how' in relation to your objective. Please consider the following factors when formulating goals;

Please elucidate your objectives; articulate the desired outcome.

Why: Comprehend the underlying motivation or purpose propelling this objective.

Please delineate the necessary procedures and resources required to achieve this objective.

For instance, if one's objective is centeredaround enhancing their professional trajectory, a clearly defined aspiration could entail attaining a higher position as a Senior Project Manager over the course of the upcoming year by obtaining advanced project management certifications.

The Quantifiability of Objectives; The Importance of Being 'SMART'

Objectives are those that can be measured in quantifiable terms and possess specific criteria for monitoring progress. They provide the opportunity to address inquiries regarding the quantity or amount involved. What is the quantity or numerical value?\\\" When formulating your objectives to be measurable, take into account the various factors;

Quantify; Establish a method to effectively ascertain and evaluate the measurable aspects of your progress.

Benchmark: Set a precedent or standard from which to measure and evaluate.

Establishing milestones is crucial; Divide your objective into manageable stages.

Illustration: One instance of a goal that can be quantified is to improve one's physical condition. A feasible aim in this regard would be to lose 20 pounds within a span of six months, while diligently monitoring progress on a weekly basis by recording body measurements and capturing photographs.

Attainable; The "A" in SMART

A realistic and achievable objective. It is crucial to set objectives that are both demanding and attainable. Kindly consider the subsequent principles when establishing goals;

Conduct a comprehensive examination of the available resources, including the allocation of time, assessment of requisite skills, and evaluation of the necessary resources.

Take into account any limitations; carefully consider factors, including obstacles and constraints.

Seek equilibrium by endeavoring for progress while upholding the attainability of the objective.

For instance, establishing an objective may entail aiming to "attain billionaire status within a 12-month timeframe." Conversely, a feasible goal could involve "enhancing one's earnings by 20% utilizing a combination of salary increments, freelancing endeavors, and prudent investment strategies."

Significance; The Value of Being SMART

Objectives are those that correspond with your deeply-held principles, aspirations, and comprehensive life strategy. They ought to be coherent within the framework of your stated goals. Facilitate the development of your individual self-improvement. During the evaluation of goal significance, take into account the following elements:

Temporal Constraints: The Significance of Establishing Time Frames

Time-limited objectives are accompanied by specific timeframes or target dates. Setting a time frame fosters a sense of urgency, alleviates the tendency to delay, and guarantees the maintenance of responsibility. When determining deadlines for your objectives, take into account the following factors;

Setting a Time Frame: Determine the desired timeline for goal attainment.

Divide your long-term objectives into specific, time-oriented milestones in order to establish clear deadlines.

Assess your progress by examining your performance in correlation with the predetermined timeline.

As an illustration, let's consider the example where your aim is to "Write a novel." To formalize this objective, you could rephrase it as follows: "Accomplish the completion of a 60,000-word novel draft within a one-year timeframe."

Does Every Action You Take Essentially Become An Ongoing Struggle To Keep Pace?

If you frequently perceive your endeavors as an ongoing struggle or consistently encounter obstacles in the completion of tasks and accomplishment of set objectives, it is recommended that you consider the adoption of brief periods of respite as an effective remedy.

The duration of daylight is gradually diminishing, yet the sun continues to emit its radiance ... Furthermore, you are currently situated indoors, attending to your professional responsibilities. In contrast to the younger generation's experience of long summer days stretching out for weeks on end and autumn symbolizing fresh beginnings, the adult perspective entails a greater degree of responsibility and multiple tasks to manage. The demands of work persist as the recent upheaval in school schedules disrupts deadlines, and the demands placed by family increase.

A balance between diligent effort and rejuvenating leisure is indispensable for achieving peak performance, in addition to fostering sound mental well-being. If you do not have the privilege of an extended eight-week sabbatical, as you did during your childhood, incorporate small respites into your daily routine. Here\\\'s how:

Soak up the change. Maximize the utilization of the available light by engaging in outdoor activities. Have a walking meeting. Rest on the verdant turf during the midday respite. Eat outside. Notice the leaves changing.

Practice boredom. Consider the hypothetical scenario wherein you decide to assume, if only for a brief span of 15 minutes, a state of mind where the perception of having no tasks or obligations exists. In the absence of continual diversion, the faculty of imagination is stimulated. The brain undergoes a reset process while the body enters a state of relaxation.

Be all in. When engaging in a task, approach it with a singular focus and commitment as if it were the sole task at hand. All things have their appointed time and season. What if responding to an email with undivided attention held the same significance and deserved the same level of concentration as conducting a meeting? Use attention wholeheartedly.

Seize the opportunity when it presents itself. The final days of summer provide a period of transition. Engage in social interactions with fellow residents on your premises. Have a BBQ. Indulge in the exquisite flavors of locally sourced butternut squash from a nearby farm. Illuminate a fire in your designated fire pit, delicately brown marshmallows over the flames, and observe as the glowing ashes gracefully drift away.

Play at work. Be less serious. Elevate the atmosphere by introducing a beach ball during a meeting. Commence the day by playing a musical composition from the Beach Boys. Commute to your workplace by riding your bicycle.

See the flowers. There is an abundance of beauty to behold in this particular season, characterized by its distinctive transformations and transitions. Mark the occasion by assimilating it. Gently come into contact with a flower while making your way from your vehicle to the workplace. Observe the cerulean heavens. Savor the warmth against your skin. Embrace the opportunity for a digital retreat during your vacations and weekends. The functioning of the world will not disintegrate if you disconnect from online platforms.

Both Putting Things Off And Avoiding Them

At some point or another in our lives, each of us has been guilty of putting things off until later. It's a fairly typical pattern of behavior, but it has the potential to wreak havoc on our productivity and steal us of valuable time. Fear of failing or a lack of drive are common causes of procrastination, but the results of this behavior can have severe repercussions. We are able to take action to free ourselves from the habits of procrastination and avoidance if we first get an awareness of the stages involved in these behaviors.

Phase 1: The Waiting Game

The first step in the process of putting things off is delaying them. We are aware that there is a task for us to finish, yet we put it off until a later time. This behavior may result in greater stress and anxiety as the due date draws closer, making it more difficult to concentrate on the task at hand and accomplish it successfully. The division of a task into a series of smaller, more manageable parts is one strategy for reducing delays. We can lessen the feeling of being overwhelmed and make progress toward our objective if we concentrate on tackling one manageable part at a time.

Distraction, the second stage

The next step in procrastination is to distract oneself from the task at hand. It's possible that we'll get started on the task at hand, but then rapidly find ourselves preoccupied with something else. This distraction could come in the shape of social media, email, or any number of other activities that are not vital. Eliminating the factor that contributes to distraction is essential if one is to be successful in overcoming it. This may include turning off notifications, scheduling certain times to check email or social media, or working in an atmosphere that is free from distractions.

Disinterest, the third stage

Disinterest is the third and last stage of the procrastination process. It's possible that we won't care about the task at hand any more after getting to this point. This loss of interest can be caused by a multitude of circumstances, such as a lack of connection to the activity or a perception that the intricacy of the task is too much to handle. It is necessary to relate the activity at hand to a larger picture in order to prevent people from becoming disinterested. Ask yourself how the successful completion of the task will contribute to the achievement of your goals and how it will benefit you in the long run.

Stage 4: The Denying Stage

The final step of procrastination is denial, which comes after three other stages. At this juncture, we might be able to persuade ourselves that the activity is not significant or that we do not possess the abilities necessary to do it. This kind of self-doubt can be paralyzing and stop us from making progress toward our objectives. It is necessary to accept our concerns and doubts and then challenge them with positive affirmations if we are going to be successful in overcoming denial. Remind yourself that you are capable of attaining your goals, as well as the significance of the task that you are currently working on.

The Realities And The Unrealistic Predictions

"We like to give people the freedom to work wherever they want (no more 9-5 mentality), secure in the knowledge that they have the drive and expertise to perform excellently, whether they are at their desk or in their kitchen. We don't have a 9-5 mentality anymore." Yours truly has never worked out of an office, nor do I want to start doing so in the foreseeable future. It was Richard Branson.

Conquering Apprehensions and Adapting Quickly to Changes in the Workplace

The world is always changing, and this includes both the ways in which we conduct our personal and professional lives. Our work ethics, norms, and procedures are always evolving to keep up with the latest technological developments. Despite this, we frequently fail to see or adjust to the changes that are occurring.

Working remotely is another stepping stone on the path we're traveling through life, and if we approach it with an optimistic perspective, we can reap many of the benefits it offers.

Changing Attitudes Toward the Work Environment

Employees now are more discerning than in the past, giving preference to companies that recognize and appreciate their efforts, time, and effort. The epidemic hastened the transition to work that can be done from home, which presents early difficulties such as juggling work and the obligations of caring for children. As the conditions have gotten better, remote workers have discovered a better work-life balance, which has made them unwilling to return to the working methods that were prevalent before the pandemic.

Why do some companies continue to ignore the changing needs of their employees?

Because of common misunderstandings, several businesses are hesitant to fully embrace the concept of remote labor. Let's bust a few of these urban legends, shall we?

Myth 1: In order for Employees to Be Productive, Constant Supervision Is Required

Despite the fact that this misconception is held by a number of companies and managers, there are only a select few people that require regular monitoring.

Many workers in today's workforce have well-defined objectives and are enthusiastic about their jobs. Because of this, people can be productive without the need for constant micromanagement. This is exemplified by the emergence of freelancers and other forms of remote labor, in which employees frequently lack direct supervision. When working remotely, people are still able to be productive and conscientious in their work.

Myth 2: Working from home is a barrier to creative and innovative thinking.

It's a common misconception, yet working from home can actually be good for your creativity and ingenuity. Employees are better able to produce original ideas when they are not subjected to the pressure that comes with working in an office setting. The dynamics of the workplace may create barriers that prevent employees from coming up with ideas, presenting their solutions, or having their ideas receive the right attention.

Myth 3: Working from a remote location makes it difficult to communicate and collaborate with others

Recent years have demonstrated that it is feasible to collaborate even when members of a team are not physically present, contrary to the beliefs of some individuals who believe that working with colleagues who are physically absent is difficult. Employees are still able to collaborate successfully despite the fact that they live in different time zones and speak different languages.

Because of advances in technology, communication technologies have made it much simpler than ever before for workers who are located in different locations to maintain connections with one another, conduct interviews, and take part in meetings online. In the modern world, communication is an obstacle that can be overcome, and it is one that teams can easily overcome if they have the right tools and the correct mindset.

Which Time Management and Productivity Improving Principles and Strategies Have Been Demonstrated to Be the Most Effective?

In this chapter, you will learn: Some of the most successful principles and tactics for increasing your time management and productivity skills. These ideas and strategies are employed by a wide variety of people.

Some instances and case studies of how these concepts and methods have worked for successful people or organizations. Instructions on how to apply these strategies and principles to various aspects of your life, such as your career, your studies, your home, your health, and your hobbies, among other things.

Which Time Management and Productivity Improving Principles and

Strategies Have Been Demonstrated to Be the Most Effective?

Your capacity for effective time management and increased productivity can be improved using a variety of different tactics and ideas. However, it's possible that not all of them will work for you or be appropriate for your circumstances. As a result, you must engage in some trial and error in order to determine what approaches yield the best results for you.

You might find success by applying some or all of the following tactics and ideas, which are among the most commonly utilized and successful in their respective fields:

Using the SMART method to set goals: Specific, Measurable, Achievable, Relevant (Realistic), and Time-bound are the components that make up the acronym SMART. These are the factors that will determine whether or not your goals are attainable, specific, and measurable. You can improve your ability to concentrate on what you want to accomplish, how you will accomplish it, and when you will accomplish it by setting SMART goals. Additionally, it might assist you in breaking down your objectives into more attainable and manageable phases.

Putting tasks in order of importance: The process of determining which tasks are more important or urgent than others and completing those chores first is referred to as prioritizing the tasks. Setting priorities for your job can help you make better use of your time, prevent you from wasting time on meaningless or unimportant tasks, and lower the stress generated by impending deadlines or an overwhelming amount of work. Putting tasks in order of importance can be accomplished using a variety of approaches, such as the ABCD analysis, the Priority Matrix, or the Eisenhower Method.

Planning ahead: Planning ahead entails making preparations in advance for the activities or objectives you have. If you plan ahead, you will be able to better organize your time, anticipate future issues or possibilities, and prevent procrastination as well as the rush that comes with waiting until the last minute. A variety of tools, including as calendars, timetables, action plans, checklists, and so on, can be utilized in the process of preparing ahead.

Delegating duties and responsibilities to other people who are more capable of doing them in a shorter amount of time or with greater accuracy than you is what is meant by the terms "delegating" and "outsourcing." You can save time, energy, and resources by delegating and outsourcing tasks, as well as concentrate on your most important responsibilities and priorities and take use of the knowledge and experience of others. Tasks can be delegated or outsourced in a variety of ways, including through the employment of freelancers, contractors, or agencies; the utilization of internet platforms or services; the solicitation of assistance from coworkers, family members, or friends; and so on.

Batching and automating: Batching and automating refer to the practice of gathering together tasks that are either similar or repetitive and completing them all at once or with very little human involvement. The use of batching and automation can help you decrease the number of interruptions, diversions, or switching expenses, as well as improve the efficiency, consistency, or quality of your work, and free up more time for jobs that require more creativity or strategic thinking. There are a variety of approaches to automating or batch processing processes, including the utilization of applications, software, or tools; the development of templates, scripts, or workflows; and the configuration of rules, alerts, or reminders.

Eliminating Distractions Getting rid of distractions is getting rid of anything that takes your attention or interest away from the work you need to get done. By getting rid of distractions, you can improve your ability to concentrate, your motivation, or the quality of the work you do; you can also cut down on errors, mistakes, or rework; and you can reach a state of flow or your peak level of performance. There are many various strategies to get rid of distractions, such as turning off notifications, messages, or calls; closing superfluous tabs, windows, or applications; donning headphones, earplugs, or noise-cancelling devices; cleaning your desk, workspace, or environment; or establishing boundaries with other people.

The Practice Of Effective Time Management

Strategies to transform time management into ingrained habits
Efficient utilization of time is imperative for fostering productivity, be it in one's personal or professional endeavors. Implementing effective time management strategies can prove to be highly advantageous. However, in order to fully capitalize on their advantages, it is imperative to incorporate these strategies into our daily routine. What is

the significance of this transition from strategic planning to habitual behavior? Habits are consistent patterns of behavior that we engage in unconsciously, requiring minimal conscious effort. They serve the dual purpose of conserving our energy and enabling long-term productivity.

Initially, the integration of time management strategies into our everyday regimen as habitual practices may appear formidable. Nevertheless, by adopting an appropriate approach, we can facilitate this transition. Subsequently, we will provide an extensive manual elucidating the process of attaining this objective.

Deliberate on your time management approaches: The initial stage in ingraining a time management strategy as a habit is to comprehensively grasp the approaches you employ. Please analyze and document all existing and prospective strategies, ensuring they remain at the forefront of your mind as you commence the cultivation of your routines.

Establish your goals: A strategy develops into a routine when it possesses a distinct intention. Specify the objectives you intend to accomplish through each time management strategy. Would you prefer to increase your productivity, decrease stress levels, gain additional free time, or achieve all of the aforementioned benefits? The establishment of a distinct objective will serve as a catalyst for maintaining motivation throughout the process of habit formation.

Establish cues: Our ingrained behaviors are instinctive reactions to stimuli in our surroundings. By linking your time management strategies with distinctive cues, you can facilitate their transformation into ingrained habits. As an illustration, in the case of having a strategy centeredaround tackling challenging tasks in the morning, an appropriate cue could be the consumption of your initial cup of coffee at the start of the day.

Embrace regularity: The act of repeating tasks is paramount in establishing a habit. Please ensure the consistent implementation of your time management strategies on a daily basis, or as scheduled, in order to reinforce this behavior until it is engrained into your routine.

Subject to positive reinforcement, our brains exhibit favorable responses to rewards, thereby strengthening the development of habits. Whenever you implement a time management strategy, it is recommended to grant yourself a modest reward. This could be as uncomplicated as a brief interlude of relaxation, a beloved indulgence, or even a mere minute to commemorate your achievement.

Embrace hurdles: The establishment of habits is a gradual process, and encountering setbacks is a natural part of it. In the event that you should happen to not implement a time management strategy on a certain day, refrain from being too hard on yourself. Alternatively, one should recognize the setback, thoroughly comprehend its cause and ways to avert it in subsequent instances, and proceed forward.

guarantees the backing of others: The presence of support from acquaintances, loved ones, or peers can serve as a compelling incentive to transform time management strategies into lasting routines. Take into consideration the possibility of discussing your objectives and tactics with a trustworthy individual, as they could potentially provide you with valuable assistance and guidance.

Assess and modify: As you endeavor to transform your strategies for time management into ingrained habits, routinely assess your progress. Inquire whether these strategies are transitioning into automatic behaviors, and if not, adapt your approach accordingly.

In summary, the shift from implementing time management strategies to embedding them as habitual practices is a gradual undertaking that necessitates diligent effort and perseverance. However, by adhering to these guidelines, you can facilitate the process of habit formation and optimize the advantages of your time management tactics. Please ensure that you proceed gradually, acknowledge your achievements, and make necessary adjustments as warranted. By displaying commitment and maintaining regularity, you will eventually discover yourself effortlessly executing these strategies, thereby liberating your mind to concentrate on other vital facets of your life.

Chapter 5
Developing Efficient Time Management Practices
Inculcating self-discipline and driving one's own motivation is integral to

developing effective time management skills. Set forth explicit guidelines and assume responsibility for your conduct in order to cultivate self-control. Establish a comprehensive timetable and exercise disciplined commitment towards it, resisting all temptations or distractions. Discover alternative methods to enhance self-motivation that resonate with your inner self, such as engaging in mental imagery to envision the advantages of accomplishing your objectives or acknowledging the negative consequences resulting from inadequate time management. One can uphold their dedication to achieving effective time management by cultivating discipline and intrinsic motivation.

Surmounting the state of analytical indecision and excessive pursuit of perfection

Perfectionism and analysis paralysis might impede your efforts to effectively manage your time. Aspire to achieve excellence, yet comprehend that attaining perfection is often unattainable and may lead to the squandering of time on inconsequential matters. Acquire the capability to effectively allocate work tasks and exercise sound judgment in decision-making. Establish sensible expectations and acknowledge that the pursuit of knowledge is a gradual journey that inevitably involves errors and imperfections. Impose temporal limitations on the decision-making process and focus on obtaining pivotal information for informed decision-making in order to prevent the occurrence of analysis paralysis. One can enhance their time management skills and avoid getting stuck in unproductive patterns by overcoming tendencies towards perfectionism and analysis paralysis.

Establishing a well-structured morning routine sets the groundwork for a productive and prosperous day ahead. Establish a comprehensive timetable encompassing activities that invigorate and prepare you for the day ahead.

Commence your daily routine by engaging in physical exercises, practicing meditation, or devoting time to journaling, all of which contribute to the enhancement of your well-being, encompassing both physical and mental aspects. Engage in prioritization of tasks, evaluate your objectives, and strategize your daily schedule. One can establish a morning ritual in order to commence the day optimally, fostering an environment conducive to maintaining concentration and achieving productivity.

Utilizing efficient time allocation strategies during periods of inactivity and idle moments

Time management skills have practical applications beyond the confines of professional environments. In order to replenish energy levels and enhance productivity, it is advisable to employ breaks and idle periods judiciously. Maximize short breaks between tasks to relax, engage in gentle physical activity or participate in a quick rejuvenating endeavor. Participate in pursuits that promote relaxation or personal growth during extended periods of respite.

Chapter 1: Establish Task Prioritization as a Core Principle

1.1 Recognizing the Significance of Prioritization

In a contemporary society characterized by an incessant influx of information, an abundance of tasks, and a multitude of responsibilities, individuals often find themselves susceptible to a sense of being overwhelmed, making it challenging to effectively manage and regulate their allocation of time. This is where the act of prioritization assumes critical importance. By assigning priority, we acquire the ability to discern the tasks of utmost significance that merit immediate attention. This, in turn, allows us to optimize the utilization of our finite time and energy resources.

The Importance of Prioritization:

1. Alleviates stress and anxiety: By attaining lucidity in prioritization, we are enabled to dedicate our attention to

sequentially accomplishing tasks, rather than becoming overwhelmed by the simultaneous burden of numerous tasks. This diminishes stress and anxiety levels, and engenders a greater sense of self-mastery.

2. Enhances productivity: Through prioritization, we are able to discern and focus on the tasks that carry significant importance and provide the greatest contribution towards achieving our objectives. Through prioritizing these tasks, we can attain more substantial outcomes within the designated time frame and level of exertion.

3. Enhances decision-making capabilities: Through the act of prioritization, we cultivate the capacity to make informed and effective decisions, spanning across various aspects of our personal and occupational spheres. This proficiency aids us in adeptly maneuvering intricate circumstances and discerning the optimal path to take.

4. Improves time management capabilities: Placing importance on prioritization forms the foundation of efficient time management. Once we gain knowledge of the tasks that hold the utmost significance, we can optimize our time allocation in a more efficient manner, thereby guaranteeing that the tasks of utmost priority are granted the requisite attention.

5. Attains an improved equilibrium between work and personal life: By employing the strategy of prioritization, we are able to discern between essential tasks and those that can be deferred or potentially removed. This affords us an opportunity to achieve equilibrium between our personal and professional spheres, thereby ensuring that we dedicate sufficient time to self-care, interpersonal connections, and recreational pursuits.

In the subsequent subsections, we shall delve into diverse methodologies and strategies that can assist you in efficiently allocating priorities to your tasks, thereby optimizing temporal utilization.

Implementing ThePomodoro Methodology For Efficient Time Allocation

The Pomodoro Technique is a widely recognized time management approach that has been proven effective in enhancing productivity and optimizing task completion within shorter time frames. The methodology is derived from the concept of subdividing one's tasks into concise, concentrated periods known as 'Pomodoros'.

Allow me to elucidate the methodology behind the Pomodoro Technique:

Please initiate a timer with a duration of 25 minutes. Throughout this duration, give undivided attention to a singular task.

After the expiration of the timer, allocate a brief interval of 5 minutes for respite. During this interval, you have the opportunity to engage in stretching exercises, hydrate yourself, or partake in other activities conducive to mental rejuvenation.

Duplicate steps 1 and 2 for a total of four intervals, subsequent to which allocate a lengthier intermission of 15-30 minutes.

Maintain a record of the number of Pomodoros accomplished on a daily basis and employ it as a gauge of your productivity.

The Pomodoro Technique is an effective method to enhance productivity as it aids in maintaining concentration while mitigating any potential interruptions. The brief intervals serve to mitigate the risk of burnout and maintain a state of rejuvenation. The methodology is applicable to a wide array of tasks, including but not limited to professional obligations, domestic responsibilities, educational endeavors, and numerous others.

Take, for instance, the hypothetical scenario in which you assume the role of a software developer who is faced with a prescribed timeframe within which to complete a project. The

PomodoroTechnique can be employed to divide your work into shorter time intervals. One may opt to allocate a duration of 25 minutes and devote their complete attention to coding during this period by utilizing a timer. After the expiration of the timer, you may avail yourself of a brief respite lasting 5 minutes. You may proceed to replicate this procedure for four intervals, after which it is advisable to allocate a lengthier interval of 15-30 minutes for rest. By employing this approach, you will attain a heightened level of concentration, effectively minimizing external disruptions, thus enhancing your efficiency and enabling you to successfully meet your deadline.

To recapitulate, the Pomodoro Technique is a straightforward yet efficacious time management strategy that can enhance productivity and facilitate accomplishing more tasks within a shorter time frame. By decomposing your tasks into shorter, targeted time blocks and incorporating regular intervals of rest, you can maintain concentration, minimize disruptions, and enhance your overall work efficiency.

Chapter 6: Multi-tasking

M
Multitasking refers to the simultaneous execution of multiple tasks. While it may appear to enhance productivity, it can, in fact, result in diminishing efficiency and escalating stress levels. Within the confines of this chapter, we shall elucidate the advantageous and disadvantageous aspects of multitasking, while concurrently presenting methodologies to proficiently handle a plethora of tasks.

Multitasking entails the aptitude to concurrently engage in multiple tasks. It is frequently regarded as a valuable skill, as it enables individuals to achieve greater productivity within shorter timeframes. Nevertheless, the act of multitasking can impede the efficiency of time management. Presented below are several strategies for effectively multitasking and enhancing efficiency in the realm of time management:

Give priority to tasks: Granting priority to tasks is essential for optimizing multitasking efficiency. Create a comprehensive task inventory and establish their order of priority in accordance with their significance and time-sensitivity. This enables you to concentrate on the key responsibilities and execute multitasking with efficiency.

Consolidate comparable tasks: Consolidating tasks that share similarities can be an effective strategy for enhancing efficiency in multitasking. As an illustration, if it is necessary to conduct telephone conversations, it is recommended to allocate a designated time period to efficiently complete all the calls in sequence. This grants you the ability to remain focused and accomplish tasks with greater efficiency.

Utilize technology: The utilization of technology can serve as a potent instrument for enhancing the efficiency of multitasking. Utilize productivity tools, such as task management software, to enhance organizational skills and effectively handle tasks. Utilize various communication mechanisms, such as instant messaging and electronic mail, to establish and maintain connections with colleagues and clients while simultaneously attending to other work responsibilities.

Minimize disruptions: The presence of distractions can greatly impede the effectiveness of multitasking. Identify prevalent sources of disruptions and endeavor to eliminate or minimize their impact as considerably as feasible. This could entail disabling the notifications on your mobile device, closing superfluous browser tabs on your computer, or seeking out a serene environment conducive to productivity.

Understanding your boundaries: It is imperative to be conscious of your limitations when engaging in multitasking. By attempting to multitask excessively, one runs the risk of committing errors and diminishing overall efficiency. Exercise pragmatism in assessing the extent of tasks you can undertake simultaneously, while actively refraining from burdening yourself excessively.

Engage in periodic intervals of rest: The act of taking breaks is essential in enhancing efficiency when multitasking. It facilitates a process of rejuvenation and concentration, enhancing your level of productivity and efficacy. Ensure to allocate scheduled intervals throughout the day and utilize them for the purpose of resting, unwinding, and replenishing one's energy.

Develop proficiency in transitioning between tasks: The ability to seamlessly transition between tasks is imperative for optimizing multitasking efficiency. Please ensure that you finish one task prior to commencing the next, while minimizing excessive task switching or frequent alternation between tasks. This facilitates the maintenance of concentration levels, ultimately leading to enhanced productivity in task completion.

To sum up, employing multitasking as a technique to enhance time management can yield significant benefits, yet it necessitates meticulous preparation and implementation. Through the establishment of task priorities, the grouping of tasks based on similarity, the utilization of advanced technologies, the conscious avoidance of distractions, the recognition of personal limitations, the integration of regular breaks, and the acquisition of adeptness in task switching, individuals can enhance their proficiency in multitasking and successfully accomplish their objectives. It is imperative to consistently reassess and modify your strategies to align with your present objectives and aspirations.

In the subsequent section, we shall examine the significance of task delegation and the methods to effectively assign tasks.

Blocking Out Time

The practice of allocating distinct chunks of time to various responsibilities or pursuits is known as time blocking, and it is one of the more common time management strategies. Managing your time and increasing your productivity with the help of this straightforward method is a breeze.

The following are some suggestions that can help you incorporate time blocking into your everyday routine:

Identify the tasks that need to be done
The first stage in the time blocking process is to determine the tasks that need to be finished. Create a list of every

single thing, no matter how big or how tiny, that needs to get done.

Set priorities for your tasks: Set priorities for your tasks depending on the importance and urgency of their completion. This will assist you in concentrating on the most important tasks and ensuring that they are finished within the allotted time.

Set aside time for each activity: Set aside a certain amount of time for each activity that is on your to-do list. Consider how long each work will actually take you, based on your experience, and adapt your timetable accordingly.

Create a timetable for your day after you have determined how much time to devote to each activity and after you have done so. This schedule ought to include specified blocks of time for each job, in addition to any breaks or downtime that may be necessary.

Maintain your routine: Maintaining as much of your routine as possible is one of the most important things you can do. This involves beginning and finishing duties at the designated times and avoiding distractions within the time allotted for work.

Maintain your routine, but don't forget that it's equally as crucial to be adaptable to any changes that may occur. It is possible that unanticipated incidents or unexpected situations will take place, in which case you may need to change your timetable accordingly.

It is essential to routinely examine your schedule and make adjustments as required. It is also important to review your schedule on a regular basis. This may require rearranging the order in which chores are completed or modifying your calendar to make room for additional commitments or activities.

The practice of time blocking has a number of advantages for efficient time management, as will be discussed further below. The following is a list of some of the benefits:

Productivity is increased because time blocking enables you to focus on one activity at a time, which, in turn, reduces the likelihood of being sidetracked by other activities.

You will be able to better manage your time and prevent procrastination if you divide your day into discrete chunks of time and devote that amount of time to each of your responsibilities.

Reduces stress Time blocking can help decrease stress since it provides you with a clear strategy for your day and lessens the feeling that you are being swamped by various responsibilities.

Accountability is improved because time blocking forces you to take responsibility for how you use your time and helps you remain focused on completing the tasks at hand.

Benefits your work-life balance When you schedule defined blocks of time for both work-related and personal tasks, time blocking can assist you in better balancing the demands of your professional and personal lives.

In conclusion, time blocking is a simple yet effective approach for time management that can assist you in managing your time more successfully and increasing the amount of work that you get done.

You may increase your productivity and get closer to achieving your goals by first determining the tasks you need to complete, then ranking those tasks in order of importance, determining how much time you will need to spend on each activity, developing a timetable, adhering to that schedule, maintaining some degree of flexibility, and reviewing your schedule on a frequent basis.

Don't forget to keep a practical outlook on your agenda and to adapt it as needed to ensure that it accurately reflects your most pressing concerns and long-term objectives.

In the next paragraph, we will talk about how to handle meetings and get the most out of the time you spend in them.

2. The Mosquito That Couldn't Remember Its Own Name

I believe I read this story in the Telugu textbook I used in either Class I or Class II. It was originally a chapter in the Telugu collection of children's stories known as PedarasiPeddamaKathalu. The first two words signify, "the poor old aunt" in their literal sense. It is a reference to an elderly woman in the fables who is depicted to be living by herself but is still able to triumph over smart and crafty foes using her wit. Examples of such foes include sly foxes and wily tigers.

There was once a fly that was known for doing a lot of work and for lending a helping hand to those around him. During one of the days of the event, the fly was buzzing around the goodies. It seemed as though the fly had completely forgotten its own name all of a sudden.

It puzzled over the question, "What is my name?" It flew a long distance without stopping and questioned everyone in the vicinity.

At some point, the fly came upon an elderly woman (pedarasipeddama) who was sitting beneath a tree. It paused at that location and questioned her, "Do you know my name?"

The elderly woman responded by saying, "I do not know your name. Why don't you ask my daughter's boyfriend?'

The fly then flew to the son of the elderly woman and questioned him, "Do you know my name?"

"I am not familiar with your name. "Ask the axe that I'm holding in my hand," the son said.

Therefore, the fly flew over to the axe and inquired, "Oh, axe of the old lady's son, do you know what my name is?"

"I am not familiar with your name. "Ask the tree that I just chopped down," remarked the axe once it had finished its work.

The fly eventually made its way to the tree. "Are you familiar with my name?"

"I am not familiar with your name. The tree responded by saying, "Ask the birds that are sitting on my branches."

The fly approached the birds that were perched on the tree and inquired, "Do you know my name?"

"We are not familiar with your name. In response to your question, the birds responded, "Ask the lake where we drink water."

This was done by the fly. "Oh, water from the lake, do you recognize my name?"

"I am not familiar with your name. In response, the lake suggested, "Ask the fish that swim in me."

Oh my goodness, there are fish swimming in the water! The fly inquired, "Do you know what my name is?"

"I am not familiar with your name. In response, the fish exclaimed, "Ask the youngster who is attempting to catch me!"

The fly approached the youngster and questioned him, saying, "Oh, you little boy who is always trying to catch fish!" Do you recognize me by my name?'

"I have no idea what your name is!" In response, the young rider said, "Ask the horse that I ride."

"Oh, you poor horse! " The fly inquired, "Do you know what my name is?" By that time, it had started to feel exhausted.

"No, I don't remember your name!" the horse said in response. Ask the baby horse that is currently growing inside of me!

"Oh, you cute little foal! "Do you know my name?" the fly, who was beginning to feel fatigued, inquired.

The infant retorted, "Your name is f...f...f...f...,"The young horse was at a loss for words and bumbled his responses instead.

After hearing it, the fly responded with an eager "Oh!" You are correct, my name is Fly, thank you.' And the fly went on its merry way back to its nest.

Acquiring An Understanding Of The Why

It is essential to gain an understanding of the factors that are contributing to your tardiness in order to create solutions that are long-lasting. This may be due to a lack of organization, putting things off till later, or having an unrealistically positive outlook on how you will handle your time. These tendencies can be made worse by ADHD, but treating the underlying issues will be essential to effecting improvement in the patient.

The fact that many adults who have ADHD have a propensity toward persistent tardiness can be related to a number of difficulties that are connected with the illness. To begin, ADHD can have an effect on "time perception," which makes it difficult for adults with ADHD to provide an accurate estimate of the amount of time it will take to accomplish a task. Second, "distractibility" is a prevalent problem; this means that their attention is quickly diverted by external stimuli, which can result in delays. Third, "procrastination" is another difficulty that many people face. Sometimes we take on more than we can handle, which results in procrastination and, ultimately, lateness. Having a firm foundation in the form of an understanding of these specific issues of ADHD is necessary in order to design successful management solutions.

You will be able to build individualized solutions that are effective for you if you first determine the underlying causes of your chronic tardiness. You will have a far better chance of bringing about change and breaking the pattern of arriving late if you have a detailed plan laid out.

The fifth chapter is titled "Distractions, Begone!" (Victory Over the Illusion That Time Is On Your Side)

No matter who you are or what you do, you will go to the future at the rate of sixty minutes per hour. This is true regardless of the passage of time. – Charles Syme

Have you ever been so engrossed in a project or activity that it seemed to take on a life of its own, or have you ever found yourself losing track of the passage of time? It's possible that you'll start out with the best of intentions, but before you know it, hours will have passed, and you'll be left wondering where the time went. If any of this seems similar to you, it's possible that you have problems with time blindness and distractions, two common challenges for people who have ADHD.

Imagine that time blindness is like a slippery fish that you are trying to catch but it just keeps getting away from you. You may feel like you have a decent hold on it, but just when you think you do, it slips away, leaving you irritated and confused. When you are working against crucial deadlines or have important duties to perform, this can be an extremely irritating situation. You may, however, learn to keep a better hold on that "slippery fish" and manage your time in a more effective manner if you employ the appropriate tactics.

One of the first things you need to do in order to deal with time blindness is to educate yourself about what it is and how it affects you. If you are able to recognize the symptoms of time blindness, such as incorrectly calculating the amount of time required to complete activities or losing track of the passage of time while working, you can begin to take efforts to reduce the negative effects of the condition.

In the following chapter, we will talk about time blindness and the effect it has on productivity. You will have a deeper understanding of what it is, how it manifests itself in those who have ADHD, and how you might spot it in yourself. In order to make the most of your time, we will discuss various strategies for time management and arranging your responsibilities in a logical order. In addition, we will cover how to fight procrastination and perfectionism, which are two frequent challenges faced by persons with ADHD. We will investigate the underlying causes of these challenges and give you with specific methods to help you overcome them.

Even when the world around you is attempting to lure you away from what you're doing, there is a toolbox full of strategies that can help you keep your focus and handle distractions. We will walk you through everything you need to know, from leveraging the power of visualization to dividing up work into manageable chunks.

When you've finished reading this chapter, you'll have a toolbox full of useful tactics to help you fight distractions and improve your time management abilities. This will allow you to make the most of the time you have and complete the things you set out to do. You will learn actionable tactics for overcoming these barriers and holding yourself accountable after you've gone through this training. If you have these tactics under your belt, you won't be able to be stopped in your pursuit of success!

It's possible that you'll become so engrossed in a project that you won't even notice the passage of time anymore. Instead, it turns into a companion that walks you through the steps of your workflow and enables you to create the greatest possible output. You may learn to harness the power of time and make it work for you rather than against you if you are willing to put in the effort and practice this skill. So without further ado, let's get right into this chapter and get started on the road to improved time management and heightened focus, shall we?

Stay focused on just one thing at a time and stay away from multitasking.

In today's environment, where we are frequently flooded with a steady stream of work, information, and requests for our attention, the ability to multitask may appear to be one of those skills that is absolutely important. It would appear that juggling multiple responsibilities at once would be an efficient approach to deal with the mountain of work that we have. However, a significant body of evidence demonstrates that attempting to multitask in fact reduces productivity, and that instead concentrating on one activity at a time might be a significantly more productive strategy.

Contrary to what the majority of people believe, multitasking does not involve executing many tasks at the same time. Our brains are not designed to be able to focus on more than one difficult undertaking at a time. Instead, what we consider to be multitasking is more accurately referred to as task switching, which is the process of the brain swiftly shifting its concentration from one activity to another. This continuous flipping can be mentally exhausting because it demands us to continually reposition our focus and attention on a variety of different things.

When we transition between different tasks, we are subject to something that is referred to as a "switching cost" or a "switching penalty." This is a reference to the loss in productivity, time, and cognitive resources that occurs as a direct result of switching between different tasks. The act of switching might throw off our train of thought, causing us to lose concentration and increase the number of errors we make. Because the brain is continually needed to engage, disengage, and then re-engage its focus and attention, it can also lead to mental tiredness. When done over an extended period of time, chronic multitasking can also contribute to stress, fatigue, and a reduction in overall productivity.

In contrast, the practice of concentrating on one activity at a time, sometimes known as "single-tasking" or "monotasking," has been shown to significantly increase both productivity and efficiency. When we give our undivided attention to a single endeavor, we are able to make more efficient use of the cognitive resources at our disposal, which results in the production of higher-quality work in shorter amounts of time. Because we are less prone to make mistakes when our attention isn't split between multiple things, focusing on one job at a time can also help limit the number of mistakes we make.

In addition, focusing our attention on a particular task at a time might be beneficial to our mental health. We can lower our levels of stress, improve our ability to focus, and derive a greater sense of satisfaction from our job if we reduce the mental clutter that is associated with moving between tasks. In addition to this, it may cause us to become more engaged and immersed in the activities we are performing, which is a condition that psychologist MihalyCsikszentmihalyi refers to as "flow."

In conclusion, it is important to note that multitasking, despite the fact that it could appear to be an effective approach to navigate our hectic life, can frequently lead to decreased productivity as well as increased stress. On the other side, single-tasking, often known as concentrating on one thing at a time, can increase productivity while simultaneously lowering error rates and enhancing mental health. We can cultivate a more focused and productive attitude to our work by giving certain activities higher priority, removing distractions, utilizing time blocking, taking breaks at regular intervals, and practicing mindfulness. Although it may appear contradictory in our fast-paced world, single-tasking enables us to operate in line with the natural tendencies of our brains, which results in increased productivity, decreased stress, and a more enjoyable work experience. It is a useful practice that increases personal effectiveness as well as overall well-being and is worth engaging in.

The Benefits Of Effective Time Management

The practice of time blocking can yield significant advantages for both the organization as a whole and its individual workforce. The aforementioned benefits encompass, but are not restricted to the subsequent aspects:

More contented employees. When employees are granted sufficient time to accomplish their tasks, they tend to experience elevated levels of satisfaction and a decreased likelihood of experiencing occupational exhaustion.

Enhanced aptitude for innovation. Employees are capable of cultivating enhanced creativity in their professional tasks when they are not encumbered by temporal limitations, as this allows for a greater scope of cognitive capacity and vitality. It is conceivable for individuals to engage proactively with their professional responsibilities, rather than merely reacting to them in a passive manner. This fosters a sense of ingenuity and creativity.

The occurrence of absenteeism witnessed a substantial reduction. Employees who experience excessive workload and elevated stress levels are more prone to availing sick leaves and various forms of time off.

A reduction in the attrition rate of employees. Individuals are more inclined to sustain long-term employment in a role where they have acquired significant experience, thus reducing their propensity to seek alternative employment opportunities.

A rise in aggregate production. Employees who experience high levels of job satisfaction and exhibit reduced tendencies to take sick leave or absences tend to be more productive in their work.

• A reputation that is held in higher regard. • A reputation that is viewed more positively. • A reputation that is considered more advantageous.

Companies that uphold and advocate for efficient time management practices have established themselves as highly sought-after employers, consequently facilitating the recruitment and retention of valuable employees.

Efficient time management can yield supplementary benefits, encompassing the alleviation of stress.

Establishing and adhering to a devised strategy for accomplishing tasks serves to mitigate feelings of anxiety. One can recognize noticeable progress by eliminating completed tasks from their list of pending activities. As a result of this, you will not have to harbor concerns or experience distress and unease concerning the completion of tasks.

More available time

By efficiently managing your time, you will have a greater amount of leisure time to engage in the activities that make up your daily routine. Individuals who possess effective time management skills will place great importance on the chance to engage in their hobbies or undertake other personal endeavors when they have additional free time at their disposal.

An amplification of the range of alternatives

When time is efficiently managed, it gives rise to a plethora of opportunities, while minimizing the squandering of valuable moments on trifling matters. Organizations perpetually seek individuals with vital skills, including exceptional time management abilities. The competency to effectively arrange and give precedence to one's tasks is an invaluable asset for any organization.

Capacity for attaining one's objectives

Individuals who possess proficient time management skills are more adept at attaining their goals and objectives, consequently enabling them to expedite the process.

Directing attention towards tasks with significant influence, as delineated in Chapter 9: "The Pareto Principle."

Concentrating on high-impact tasks, commonly referred to as the 80/20 Rule, is an indispensable element of efficient time management that is universally applicable across diverse professions. In accordance with this theoretical framework, commonly known as the Pareto Principle, it can be posited that a mere 20% of endeavors are accountable for generating a substantial 80% of outcomes. In alternative terms, a relatively minuscule fraction of the tasks substantially contribute to the overall outcomes. This method enables individuals to concentrate their endeavors on high-impact actions that yield the most significant outcomes.

Various applications of the "80/20 Rule" include the ability to employ it in business operations to identify the most lucrative products, customers, and distribution channels. This strategy enables businesses to concentrate their marketing endeavors on tasks with substantial impact, thereby augmenting their outcomes and overall success.

● Personal Growth: When it comes to personal growth, individuals have the opportunity to employ the 80/20 principle to effectively allocate their time and effort towards activities that yield the highest levels of satisfaction and contribute to their personal betterment. This methodology prompts individuals to direct their attention towards the tasks that hold the greatest significance for them, thereby enhancing their overall quality of life.

● Time Management: Utilizing the 80/20 rule serves as a beneficial technique in the realm of time management, granting individuals the ability to discern their most consequential tasks and concentrate their endeavors towards these specific activities. This approach serves the purpose of preventing diversions, eliminating tasks of minimal importance, and refining the agenda, ultimately amplifying productivity and achieving desired outcomes.

The Psychological Basis of the Pareto Principle:

The principle of the 80/20 rule is rooted in the psychological concept of prioritizing tasks with significant impact. When individuals direct their attention towards endeavors that yield tangible outcomes and a sense of fulfillment, it establishes a constructive cycle of drive and concentration. Consequently, this results in enhanced productivity and achievement.

Suggestions for Effectively Implementing the Principle of Pareto's Law:

● Determine Your Highest Impact Assignments: To begin implementing the principles of the 80/20 rule, it is imperative to identify and ascertain the tasks that yield the greatest value. This can be achieved through an analysis of your findings and identifying the tasks that significantly contribute to your overall success.

- Emphasize Task Prioritization: Once you have discerned the tasks with significant influence, allocate priority based on their significance. This will assist you in directing your efforts towards the tasks that hold the utmost significance.
- Minimize Disturbances: Adhering to the principles of the 80/20 rule entails concentrating your attention on tasks that yield significant outcomes, thus it becomes imperative to minimize disturbances. This can be achieved through the implementation of strategies such as diminishing the quantity of tasks with low impact, mitigating interruptions, and establishing a work environment that fosters concentration.
- Establishing Timelines: Establishing timelines for your high-priority tasks can assist in maintaining concentration and drive. This strategy guarantees that you are effectively advancing towards

your objectives and assists in maintaining focus and adherence.

● Sustain High Levels of Motivation: Adherence to the 80/20 rule relies on the psychological aspect of motivation, and thus it is of utmost importance to constantly sustain high levels of motivation. This objective can be achieved through a dedicated emphasis on one's goals, commemorating accomplishments, and maintaining a constructive mindset.

In conclusion, the principle of the 80/20 rule represents a potent instrument for optimizing time allocation and enhancing productivity. This concept enables individuals to channel their energies towards tasks of paramount importance, which lead to desirable outcomes and personal fulfillment. Whether it is utilized for personal growth or in a professional setting, this principle has the ability to assist individuals in effectively organizing their tasks and enhancing their productivity and overall achievements. By incorporating the principle of the 80/20 rule into their daily lives, individuals can attain heightened levels of success and fulfillment.

www.ingramcontent.com/pod-product-compliance
Lightning Source LLC
Chambersburg PA
CBHW052136110526
44591CB00012B/1747